My Baby Brother Needs A Friend

by Jane Belk Moncure
illustrated by Frances Hook

THE CHILD'S WORLD

ELGIN, ILLINOIS 60120

Library of Congress Cataloging in Publication Data

Moncure, Jane Belk.
  My baby brother needs a friend.

  SUMMARY: A young girl describes her relationship
with her brother who is not yet one year old.
  [1. Brothers and sisters—Fiction. 2. Babies—
Fiction] I. Hook, Frances. II. Title.
PZ7.M739Mybc   [E]   78-21935
ISBN-0-89565-019-3

Distributed by Childrens Press, 1224 West Van Buren Street,
Chicago, Illinois 60607.

My
Baby
Brother
Needs
A Friend

My baby brother is still so small.
He sleeps a lot,
and hardly cries at all.
But he can kick,
and roll,
and crawl, just about everywhere.
He is still so small
he needs someone to look after him.

That's what I do.

I sing him a song
and rock him to sleep.

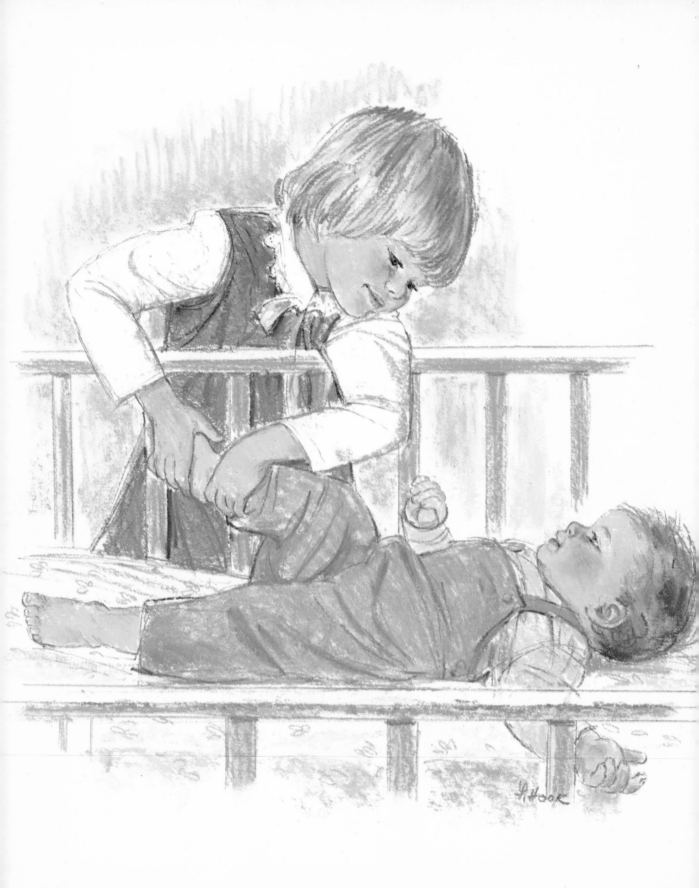

I play with him
and tickle his toes.

Sometimes I help him take a bath.
He splashes me—
but I just laugh.

Sometimes I take him for a ride.
I tell him about all the things
I see,
because he is still too little
to talk to me.
But he can smile,
and say some sounds
and wave.

He can fuss and cry,
especially when he is wet,
or hungry.

Someday he will be big enough
to walk alone.
But for now,
I will hold his hand
and help him stand.

17

When it rains,
he and I will play together
in my room.

19

When it snows,
I will catch snowflakes
for him to hold.

When we go to the zoo,
I will lift him up,
so he can see the animals too.

When we go to the park,
he can ride with me
on the merry-go-round.

He can sit in my lap
and swing.

In spring,
when my birthday comes,
guess what I will do.
I will let him come to my party
and help blow out the candles!

I will give him a piece
of my birthday cake.
You see,
he has never had a birthday of his own—
not yet.
He has never made a wish,
or blown one candle out
or opened a big surprise
from a friend.

29

He is still so small
he doesn't have many friends.
That's why he needs a friend like me.

About the Artist

Frances Hook was educated at the Pennsylvania Museum School of Art in Philadelphia, Pennsylvania. She and her husband, Richard Hook, worked together as a free-lance art team for many years, until his death. Within the past 15 years, Mrs. Hook has moved more and more into the field of book illustrating.

Mrs. Hook has a unique ability for capturing the moods and emotions of children. She has this to say about her work. "Over the years, I have centered my attention on children. I've done many portraits of children. I use children in the neighborhood for my models. I never use professional models."

A great admirer of Mary Cassatt, an American Impressionist, Mrs. Hook enjoys doing fine art as well as commercial work.

About the Author

Jane Belk Moncure, author of many books and stories for young children, is a graduate of Virginia Commonwealth University and Columbia University. She has taught nursery, kindergarten and primary children in Europe and America.

Mrs. Moncure has taught early childhood education while serving on the faculties of Virginia Commonwealth University and the University of Richmond. She was the first president of the Virginia Association for Early Childhood Education and has been recognized widely for her services to young children.

She is married to Dr. James A. Moncure, Vice President of Elon College, and lives in Burlington, North Carolina.